Mrs. P. O. Thacker
800 Hillcrest
Danville, Kentucky.

Flowers at the White House
An Informal Tour

Frontispiece: *The Jacqueline Kennedy Garden*

Flowers at the White House

An Informal Tour
of the Home
of the Presidents
of the United States

by Ruth Montgomery

M. Barrows and Company, Inc.
Distributed by William Morrow & Co., Inc.
New York, 1967

To my husband

ACKNOWLEDGMENTS

THIS BOOK was made possible through the enthusiastic cooperation of Mrs. Lyndon B. Johnson and her able press secretary, Elizabeth Carpenter, to whom I am deeply indebted for their interest and for making the necessary White House facilities available.

I would further like to express my appreciation to Homer Gruenther, a White House assistant from the beginning of the Eisenhower Administration until his retirement in 1965, who conceived the idea for this book. During the Kennedy and Johnson administrations, Mr. Gruenther directed arrangements for special tours of the White House for distinguished visitors. In this capacity, he observed that many of them found as much delight in examining the picture albums of flowers used on State occasions as in seeing the beautifully restored White House itself. Since those albums are maintained in the flower room and are not available to the public, Mr. Gruenther suggested that I prepare this book so that all Americans might enjoy at least part of this unique record.

I am grateful to White House floral designer, Elmer M. (Rusty) Young, to his assistant, James David Nelson, and to White House photographer, Robert L. Knudsen, whose combined artistry may be seen on the pages that follow. Flower photography is a decided change of pace for "Chief" Knudsen, a Navy photographer who saw camera action on Guam and on a Pacific carrier in Vietnamese and Korean waters before being assigned to the White House in 1957.

To him and other participating photographers, and also to White House curator James R. Ketchum and Marcia Maddox of the First Lady's staff, I extend my thanks. All played significant parts in producing this first published presentation of flowers at the White House.

R.M.

Washington, D.C., 1967

CONTENTS

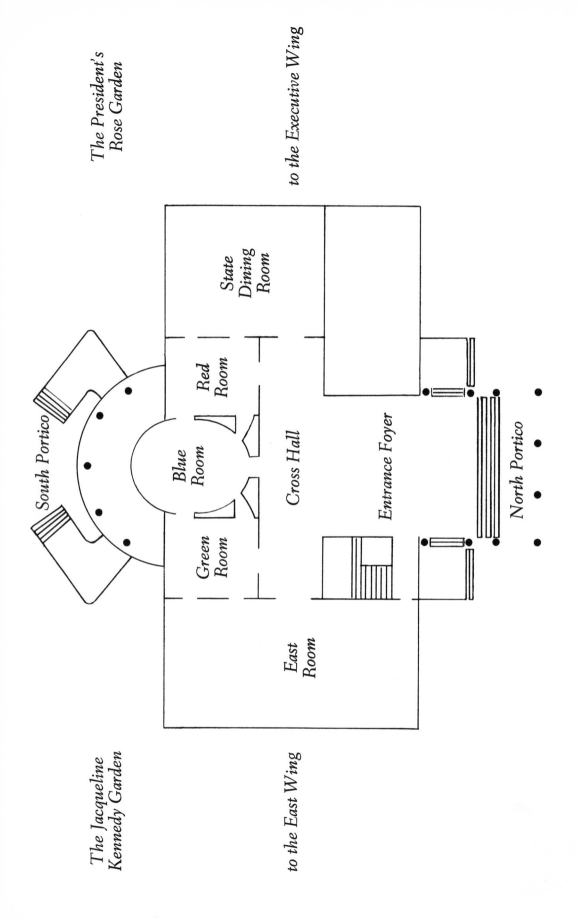

The President's
Rose Garden

to the Executive Wing

South Portico

State
Dining
Room

Red
Room

Blue
Room

Cross Hall

Green
Room

Entrance Foyer

North Portico

East
Room

The Jacqueline
Kennedy Garden

to the East Wing

Plan of THE STATE ROOMS—*First Floor*

Flowers at the White House
An Informal Tour

THE WHITE HOUSE—*South Portico*

INTRODUCTION

Unlike the official residences of the heads of state of most countries, the White House did not originate as a palace. It is indeed a most elegant and beautiful mansion, designed, however, not for royalty but for the chief executive of a new democracy. The early presidents of the United States were aristocrats, but not kings. For them the appropriate home was conceived as a great manor house, resembling those of the landed gentry of eighteenth-century England, Ireland, or France.

There are many records, past and present, on every conceivable aspect of the Executive Mansion, including details of housekeeping, decoration, or entertaining that give a fascinating picture of the White House as a working household. Among the most enchanting—and quite unprecedented—of such records are the recent albums of color photographs of flowers used in the State rooms on official occasions. Started during the Kennedy Administration, these albums show hundreds of bouquets which in their loose and uncontrived style have the look of the fresh garden flowers one would naturally expect at a great country estate. They reflect admirably the spirit in which the White House was originally designed. It is not too much to say that the use of flowers in this particular fashion is an integral part of the Kennedy restoration of the interior of the mansion that so captured the public imagination a few years ago.

But flowers are also captivating in themselves. Even in the historic settings against which they are seen in this book, these bouquets can be viewed in a personal way as flowers that could just as naturally grace one's own house. Though dozens of arrangements may be made for a State occasion in the President's House, there is no reason why just one of them could not create the same stroke of color and delight in one's own living room.

These photographs were not originally intended for publication. Their purpose was to provide a working reference manual for the White House flower room. But they prove now to be also an inspiration for all Americans, a delightful chapter in the story of the decorative arts in our country, and—because all those shown here were taken on occasions of considerable importance at the White House—they provide an unexpected, intimate footnote to contemporary history as well.

For the first time in its history, the White House now has a permanent curator, James R. Ketchum, who catalogues the valuable antiques that began to flood into the White House after Mrs. John F. Kennedy's inspirational appeal to the nation to help in its restoration. Mr. Ketchum studied at Colgate University and was graduated from George Washington University—where he majored in American history and American art—and transferred to the White House from the Custis-Lee Mansion, operated by the Interior Department, early in the Kennedy Administration. In March of 1964, President Johnson appointed him permanent curator. To the able Mr. Ketchum, who is so youthful that he gives his age only as "in the late twenties," we are indebted for delightful anecdotes about previous First Families, information on the mansion's collection of vases, bowls, and urns, and insight into the changing tastes that have reflected our gradual development from a struggling New World republic to the world's mightiest power.

IN THE PRESENT CENTURY, the White House has undergone three major renovations. The Theodore Roosevelt restoration of 1902 halted the trend for heavy and ornate Victorian décor that had begun during the Grant Administration of the 1870s and continued unabated through the McKinley era. When the ebullient Roosevelt family moved to the White House, TR's daughter "Princess" Alice recalled later in her memoirs, the furnishings were "late General Grant and early Pullman" car, the ceilings "frescoed with acres of oilcloth patterns." Congress came to their rescue with an appropriation of nearly half a million dollars, and Teddy Roosevelt ordered sweeping changes that restored the classic elegance of the Monroe era. He also ordered the destruction of the mansion's sprawling growth of greenhouses to make way for the Executive West Wing that has since served all presidents as their office quarters.

In 1948, President Truman launched the most drastic and necessary reconstruction since the burning of the White House in 1814. The mansion was in a state of near collapse and a hard-won congressional appropriation of over five million dollars made possible the complete gutting and rebuilding of the entire structure. Only the exterior walls were left standing; the details of interior architecture were laboriously dismantled, preserved, and later reinstalled. Four years passed before the First Family could return to the White House.

President Truman had hoped, too, to proceed to a refurnishing of the mansion with authentic period furniture and antiques related to the history of the White House. But the major effort to do this did not come until the Kennedy Administration. Mrs. John F. Kennedy, with the help of a committee of museum experts under the official supervision of a government Fine Arts Commission, was the moving force in a historic refurbishing of the interior of the White House that relied entirely on the contributions of private donors.

Here began today's story of flowers at the White House. Mrs. Kennedy knew her restoration project would take a long time, but she sensed that the flowers could easily be improved to such an extent that the results would be seen immediately. The loose natural arrangements that became a hallmark of the Kennedy Administration, and that are enthusiastically continued by Mrs. Johnson, contrasted sharply with the fashions of the past hundred years.

OVER A CENTURY BEFORE, during the Pierce Administration, most of the flowers for the President's House were supplied by government greenhouses, as they are today, but there the resemblance ended. The wife of Senator Cassius Clay of Kentucky wrote in the 1850s of the bouquets favored by Mrs. Franklin Pierce: "They were stiff and formal things, as big around as a breakfast plate, and invariably composed of a half-dozen wired japonicas ornamented with a pretentious cape of marvelously-wrought lace-paper. At every plate, at every state dinner, lay one of these memorable rigid bouquets." Even this may have been an improvement over the earlier administration of President James Polk, who conducted a Spartan regime during which dancing and refreshments were taboo at all soirées, while Mrs. Polk refused to use flowers grown in government conservatories because she wanted "no special privilege."

Evidently, not only changing fashions but the temperaments of its various occupants have affected the ups and downs of flowers at the White House. During Thomas Jefferson's two terms, this most creative of our presidents banked the wide windows with rare plants, his own botanical experiments; a tame mockingbird lived among the plants and rode around the mansion on the

President's shoulder. In very different spirit were the great greenhouses of the second half of the nineteenth century. Bachelor President James Buchanan was the first to build an "elegant conservatory" in the late 1850s, and succeeding presidents added more and more greenhouses that grew like Topsy until they covered acres of ground to the west of the White House. These became favorite gathering places for guests, both before and after State functions, where the Marine band played romantic airs in one corner of the conservatories while richly gowned ladies and beribboned ambassadors strolled through the maze to examine the exotic blooms.

After the death from typhoid fever of her son Willie, Mary Todd Lincoln banned all flowers from the White House because he had loved them. Before that tragedy, however, Mrs. Lincoln and other fashionable Washington ladies wore in their braided hair broad bandeaux loaded with garlands of flowers, trailing vines at the rear; bouquets were fastened to their wrists and wreaths festooned their sweeping skirts. The elaborate ornamentation of the Victorian era was already taking hold in the 1860s, and the fashion in flowers was following suit. Few presidents expended such substantial sums of money on flowers as did Chester A. Arthur some twenty years later. He often augmented the White House conservatory supply with huge orders from New York florists, and his personal floral bill for one State dinner was said to be fifteen hundred dollars. In 1886, President Grover Cleveland married Miss Frances Folsom at the White House. Though only forty relatives and friends were present at the marriage ceremony, news accounts disclosed that floral national shields were fastened to every column in the East Room, the fireplaces in all State rooms were solidly packed with flowers, mirrors were wreathed, and mantels were banked with floral monograms of the bride and groom. The youthful Mrs. Cleveland demonstrated a flair for the different shortly thereafter at State dinners honoring the Cabinet in January, 1887, and the Supreme Court the following month. The centerpiece for the first dinner was a big boat of red and white camellias; for the Court, two open books fashioned of white immortelles labeled in purple, "Book of the Law."

During the next administration, Mrs. Benjamin Harrison introduced a fad for orchids and used a staggering plethora of plants and flowers at formal parties. They came from the White House conservatories, from federal propagating gardens, and in heated vans from New York and Philadelphia. The Victorian Age of the 1890s was now in full cry, and, after redecorating the White House in a smothering pomposity of geegaws, overdrapes, and fringes, the Harrisons further disguised its once elegant simplicity with miles of smilax looped around the walls and chandeliers. A botanically-minded reporter of the times wrote

The President's Rose Garden. It is some time since this garden behind the President's office in the Executive West Wing has been a true rose garden. But, flowering in the foreground among chrysanthemums of many colors, in November of 1965, was a John F. Kennedy white rose.

that at one of the Harrison's parties the East Room alone boasted five thousand decorative plants in addition to the trailing smilax. The news account said florists had managed to crowd onto mantels and window seats two thousand azaleas, eight hundred carnations, three hundred roses, three hundred tulips, nine hundred hyacinths, four hundred lilies-of-the-valley, two hundred bouvardias, a hundred sprays of asparagus fern, forty poinsettia plants, and two hundred small ferns.

A photograph of the East Room taken during the McKinley Administration that followed also shows a busy display of horticulture, with the addition of numerous potted palms. Since the turn of the century, a complete revolution in taste has of course occurred and such excesses have long since vanished. But certain formal conventions naturally lingered on in this great house that is used for so many formal State functions. From Theodore Roosevelt through the Franklin Roosevelt years, potted palms continued to be the fashion at the White House. Conventional floral sprays of a single color were the rule in the State rooms during the Truman and Eisenhower administrations. Baker fern found their way into nearly every table decoration, and the horseshoe dining table was draped in the traditional swags of smilax.

THE REORGANIZATION of the flower room was one of the first projects undertaken by Jacqueline Kennedy after her husband's inauguration. She enlisted the help of her friend Mrs. Paul Mellon, a member of her committee for the restoration of the White House. Under the expert tutelage of Mrs. Mellon and her horticulturist, Mr. Charles Pecora, the flower-room designers began working on graceful, natural arrangements of a kind long favored in France. A wide variety of blossoms in a galaxy of colors were used, combined to reflect the colors in paintings and wall hangings in the various rooms. Gone were the Baker fern and nearly all other foliage except that which is natural to the flowers themselves. Stems cut to various lengths were used to build up the graceful curves of massed bouquets of an unaffected pre-Victorian charm.

Magnificent containers were available for them to work with, such as the remarkable collection of French bronze-doré and vermeil brought into the White House by President James Monroe in 1817 and the large Biddle collection of vermeil. The latter consists chiefly of English and French pieces covering a wide span from the Renaissance to the present. It was willed to the White House by Mrs. Margaret Thompson Biddle and became a part of the permanent White House collection in 1956.

A work plan was developed for the flower room so that after one year's run-through it could be followed in succeeding years without frantic last-minute calls to area florists to enquire about seasonal flowers. Lists were made of which containers were to be used in each room. Vermeil urns that had formerly been kept under lock and key were designated for the Red Room and the upstairs hall outside the Treaty Room. Chinese export bowls were chosen for the Green and Blue rooms and Monroe bronze-doré and vermeil pieces for the State Dining Room. Color photographs were taken of the flowers arranged for every State and official occasion, and these were captioned as to occasion, types of flowers, and date, to be used for future models.

Mrs. Kennedy believes that a room is never at its best without fresh flowers but that "too many bouquets" in a single salon must be avoided. She feels strongly that flowers in the house should look as though they came from a garden. She therefore directed that flowers suitable to the season be used at all times, with an occasional specimen variety as a focal point. In the spring she favored fruit blossoms, lilacs, hyacinths, lily-of-the-valley, freesia, ranunculus, anemones, sweet peas, iris, pussy-willow, and forsythia. Her summer preferences were sweet William, stock, heliotrope, zinnias, dahlias, geraniums, foxglove, heliopsis, calendula, roses, lilies, and peonies. For fall and winter she chose tuberoses, gerbera daisies, bouvardia, chrysanthemums, ornamental oranges, stevia, and blue lace-flower, and holly and natural greens at Christmastime. During the Kennedy Administration, flowers were kept in the State rooms at all possible times so that the hordes of tourists that visit the White House five mornings a week could see the rooms at their best. At night, the bouquets were removed and refrigerated to prolong their use.

CHIEF FLORAL DESIGNER Elmer Young began his career as a part-time florist's delivery boy while working his way through the University of Miami. Forced by lack of funds to drop out of college, he spent two years in on-the-job training at Chaplin Florists in Miami and took a course at the American School of Floral Art in Chicago in 1949. He afterwards worked as a floral arranger in Nashville, Buffalo, and Washington before joining the White House staff under head gardener Robert M. Redmond in 1953. After Mr. Redmond retired, Mrs. Kennedy personally selected Rusty Young for his present position, in August of 1962.

Mr. Young infinitely prefers today's arrangements to those of the pre-Kennedy years. From 1953 until 1961, he and other members of the staff were under

The Jacqueline Kennedy Garden. Conceived during the Kennedy Administration, it actually came into being during the Johnson Administration and was dedicated in the spring of 1965. It was designed to serve as a secluded spot where the First Lady can entertain. The beds contain seasonal flowers for cutting and herbs for the kitchen. In the background, the East Wing.

instructions to use only white flowers in the Red Room, yellow ones in the Blue Room, and lavender or pink in the Green Room. The designs were formal and symmetrical, huckleberry foliage or Baker fern were incorporated in the bouquets, and clear glass vases were ordinarily used. In the Red and Green rooms, the bouquets sat on matching tables with candelabra, at either side of mirrors on the south walls. Two small vases of flowers perched on each mantel. "Mrs. Kennedy changed all that," Mr. Young recalls. "She didn't like flowers on mantels and, after the furniture was replaced and rearranged, we could place bouquets only against the north walls and on the circular table in the center of the Blue Room. Vermeil vases and Chinese export bowls largely replaced the glass ones."

After Jacqueline Kennedy's more continental tastes became known, the State rooms sprang to life with multicolored bouquets keyed to the colors of the historic paintings and of the silk wall hangings. At first, Mrs. Kennedy used to leave her books of still-life paintings in the flower room for Mr. Young to study, but to her delight she soon discovered that this talented designer was "doing things that were even more beautiful, of his own inspiration." Mrs. Kennedy says, "He needs only a suggestion, a few words, or a few flowers held in front of a container to know how to finish an arrangement. He has an instinctive feeling for color and mass and can do bowls of flowers that look like Dutch still-lifes with whatever materials are on hand." And she found that Rusty Young was extremely talented at making flowers last and rearranging bouquets to gain the most use possible from them.

He was not afraid to experiment with new colors and found, for instance, for the Red Room—where only white flowers had previously been used because of the vivid walls—a variety of red peonies and rubrum lilies (white flecked with red) that exactly matched the new cerise hangings. Thereafter, those flowers, roses, and sometimes lavender pompons were mixed with the white flowers. The Sèvres vases on pier tables in the Cross Hall on the main floor displayed redskin chrysanthemums, red roses, and peonies to pick up the color of the maroon carpeting. The antique scenic wallpaper that Mrs. Kennedy persuaded the National Society of Interior Decorators to purchase for the Diplomatic Reception Room is a stunning backdrop for colorful assortments of red, lavender, and yellow anemones, or Duchess spoon chrysanthemums and pompons in bronzes and reds. Since the Kennedy family has donated Claude Monet's "Morning on the Seine" in memory of the late President, a low bowl on the table beneath it in the Green Room reflects the misty lavenders, purples, pinks, blues, and greens of the painting. Anemones are especially effective for this purpose.

Rusty Young likes to think that these graceful, loose bouquets which Mrs. Kennedy and Mrs. Johnson both favor are far more in keeping with the White

House than the stiff arrangements and tortured sprays of the previous hundred years. He explains that "in the early days, the gardeners not only tended the flowers but cut and arranged them as well; and you can be sure they mixed them together pretty informally."

Rusty Young's mechanics for arranging flowers are simple. Oasis, an absorbent material that comes in blocks, is his favorite means of anchoring flowers in a container. For vermeil bowls and others that are easily scratched, he ordinarily cuts a block of Oasis in half, soaks it in water, then places it in the vase and inserts the flowers one at a time. For some of the priceless Sèvres and Chinese export bowls, he first arranges the flowers in plastic pans or papier-mâché containers, using Oasis and chicken wire; then he sets these inside the bowls. He never uses needlepoint holders or clay as supports. For little vermeil beakers and porcelain jugs, he packs the flowers and greenery in tightly enough so that they hold themselves in place without Oasis or wire.

Assistant designer James Nelson recalls that Mrs. Kennedy requested small dainty arrangements for coffee tables and lamp tables. "I want this to look like a country house," she once told him. Mr. Nelson is a native Washingtonian, the adopted son of a policeman. While he was in high school, he worked as a busboy at the Mayflower Hotel and after graduation drove a delivery truck for the Mayflower Flower Shop until its manager, Mrs. Eleanor O'Neil Robertie, decided to train him as a designer. He worked there for seven years, until he applied to fill a vacancy on the White House flower-room staff and was hired in 1954. Since then, the former busboy has been designing bouquets that have been praised by presidents, kings, queens, prime ministers, cabinet ministers, and the hundreds of thousands of plain citizens who stream through the White House on public tours.

Of the Eisenhower years, Elmer Young recalls, "The President sometimes picked a rose from the garden outside his office and carried it directly to his wife in the family quarters upstairs. His favorites were the Peace roses in creams, yellow, and pink. Mrs. Eisenhower loved flowers, particularly carnations and sweetheart roses. We used to keep a big bowl of pink carnations at all times in the West Hall, where the family sat, and a glass vase of pink sweetheart roses in Mrs. Eisenhower's bedroom." Rusty Young remembers vividly that Mrs. Kennedy disliked "tight roses and wanted them fully opened" before they were used in White House bouquets. She had a definite aversion to nearly all spike flowers, preferring "the composite ones with strong centers, such as marguerite daisies and daisy-type chrysanthemums." "Mrs. Johnson's likes and dislikes in flowers are not as strong as Mrs. Kennedy's," he says, "but she expresses more enthusiasm for them than other First Ladies I have known. President Johnson, on the other hand, seems less interested in the flowers than his two predecessors. He doesn't comment on them as he passes through the flower shop en route to the swimming pool, but President Kennedy used to stop and ask the names of different flowers. Once he particularly admired some large red roses and another time he enquired about some potted cyclamen that he mistook for orchids. He liked to wear a blue bachelor's-button in the lapel of his dinner jacket, so we tried to keep a supply on hand."

ONE OF Mrs. Lyndon Johnson's first missions after moving to the White House was to call at the flower room off the garden to tell chief designer Elmer Young, "Please continue the way you've been doing the flowers. Everyone likes them." To newswomen whom she conducted on an early tour of the mansion, she exclaimed enthusiastically, "Look at the flowers. They're the most artistic thing in the house." Mrs. Johnson believes that fresh flowers in a room "give a feeling of welcome, of expectancy." They are the final touch that seems to say, "this room is ready for enjoyment."

Though Lady Bird Johnson is invariably presented with an arm-filling sheaf of "the yellow rose of Texas" wherever she goes, this is not her favorite flower. Under date of May 17, 1965, Rusty Young carefully noted that Mrs. Johnson told him her favorite blossoms are peonies; the file card further details that she "likes anemones, lily-of-the-valley, and ranunculus," and also seems to prefer "yellows, oranges, and pinks." "I have a great many favorites," she says, "but in summer there is nothing more cheerful than to see cut flowers from the garden—zinnias, marigolds, and peonies." Seasonal blossoms now are often obtained from the Jacqueline Kennedy Garden, behind the East Wing of the mansion, which was completed in 1965 during the Johnson Administration.

"I like flowers to speak of the season," Mrs. Johnson told me, "and they do at the White House. In spring, there is likely to be a huge arrangement of yellow forsythia in the East Room, or a mass of fragile blossoms such as apple, plum, or cherry. And great use is made in spring of graceful tulips in all colors, fragrant jonquils, narcissus, and perhaps pussy-willow. They all say, 'Spring is here.' In the fall, we have chrysanthemums in a great range of yellow, bronze, red, and every autumn hue. Occasionally, some wheat in the bouquet reminds one that it is harvest time. I like informal arrangements, and straw baskets are delightful containers.

"Certainly there are colors that bring out the personality or glamour of a room, just as they do for a woman. In the Red Room, I always delight to see the rubrum lilies and pink and red roses and many blending shades of red and pink that speak to the red satin of the walls and the other fabrics in the room. In the Queen's Room [upstairs], which is done in rosy tones, I love pink carnations, rubrum lilies, and pink and red roses." Eloquently praising the Claude Monet in the Green Room, Lady Bird added, "Underneath the Monet, which is a misty landscape of blues, greens, and lavenders, I usually find a blend of flowers that sings a duet with the painting." This is indeed one of the loveliest combinations of flowers and fine art at the White House.

TODAY, no trace of the earlier conservatories remain, but on the roof of the mansion, unseen by the public, is a small utility greenhouse where scented geranium leaves for finger bowls are grown. Chinese evergreens for the President's office are also nurtured there, along with a few orchid plants. Except for State dinners when masses of flowers are needed, normal requirements are met by the United States Park Service's Kenilworth Gardens located in the northeast section of Washington. Nowadays, in the State Dining Room, the Johnsons, like the Kennedys, prefer numerous round tables for ten and one rather small head table instead of the traditional U-shaped banquet table. So Rusty Young and James Nelson may create as many as a hundred separate flower arrangements to be used throughout the mansion on a State occasion. If tables are set out-of-doors, they place flowers in Oasis collars around the hurricane lamps; they then arrange a duplicate set of centerpieces for the State Dining Room in the event of rain.

The restored White House today has a certain style and beauty, an authenticity, of which Americans are very much aware. Its priceless contents can be preserved for the future, and in fact must be by recently enacted law. Fresh flowers will abide by no such law, but the camera can record some of their finest hours at the White House. Surely one of the most beautiful displays ever seen there was assembled for President and Mrs. Lyndon Johnson's dinner dance in honor of Princess Margaret and Lord Snowdon on November 17, 1965. The illustrated pages of this book open with a colorful tour of the President's House as it looked on that festive night.

The State Dining Room ready for guests.

Flowers at THE WHITE HOUSE
November 17, 1965

Lavender, yellow, and white chrysanthemums, lavender heather, yellow and white marguerite daisies, pink, yellow, and red roses and rubrum lilies—in one of a set of bamboo-design vermeil bowls donated to the White House by Mrs. Paul Mellon. All the color pictures on these pages were taken on the night of President and Mrs. Johnson's dinner dance for Princess Margaret and Lord Snowdon, on November 17, 1965.

The State Dining Room

The color photographs taken throughout the White House before this especially festive evening are the most lavish and brilliant in the flower-room albums. In the State Dining Room fourteen round tables set for ten replaced the traditional formal banquet table that had seldom been used during this or the past administration. Identical low centerpieces for each table were arranged in matching vermeil bowls. The Truman china, Kennedy crystal, and Monroe vermeil flatware were used; candles were set in contemporary frosted-glass hurricane lamps.

The Green Room

In the Green Room the night of the dinner dance, a pair of bouquets in Chinese export bowls—lavender and white stock, white and pink daisy chrysanthemums, lavender chrysanthemums and heather, lavender and purple anemones, variegated pink and white anemones, and pink carnations and disbud chrysanthemums.

The bouquets were placed against the north wall, on a matched pair of New England card tables. Lattice-back chairs attributed to Samuel McIntire. Chinese export ashtrays of the same moss green as the watered-silk hangings installed during the Kennedy restoration. Above, Claude Monet's "Morning on the Seine," given in memory of President Kennedy by his family.

The pair of bouquets in the Red Room were arranged in vermeil urns—white stock and chrysanthemums, white and lavender daisy chrysanthemums, and rubrum lilies. Gold vermeil game birds from the Margaret Biddle collection. Cerise silk wall hangings with woven gold border of the Kennedy restoration.

The Red Room.

The flowers were placed on a pair of card tables with winged sphinxes, presumed to have been made in America by the French cabinetmaker Charles Honoré Lannuier. American Empire side chairs, circa 1820; vermeil ornaments also from the Biddle collection. The portrait of Woodrow Wilson is by the noted British artist, Sir William Orpen. It was painted from life early in 1919, while the President was in France for the negotiation of the Treaty of Versailles that ended World War I.

The Library

No room in the White House was without flowers. In the Library, a quiet room on the lower floor, white carnations and stock, bronze Duchess spoon chrysanthemums, yellow pompon chrysanthemums, and bronze daisy chrysanthemums—in an antique Chinese export bowl.

FLOWERS AT THE WHITE HOUSE
November 17, 1965

THE WHITE HOUSE never glittered more elegantly than on this night of President and Mrs. Johnson's dinner dance for Princess Margaret and Lord Snowdon. One hundred and forty Very Important Personalities enjoyed a party that was indeed fit for a princess. For weeks beforehand, social secretary Bess Abell had been planning every meticulous detail. Three days in advance, floral designers Rusty Young and James Nelson began assembling masses of flowers from Park Service greenhouses and local wholesalers, which they arranged into seventy separate bouquets. Fourteen of these formed centerpieces for the round tables for ten in the State Dining Room. French chef René Verdon personally directed the kitchen staff in the task of boning 154 squab—an extra bird for each table so that no guest would have to remove the last one from a platter—and picked fresh thyme from the herb beds in the Jacqueline Kennedy Garden. The hand-written menus announced pompano amandine, the roast squab stuffed with wild rice, artichoke hearts filled with puréed peas and carrots, a salad, Brie cheese, praliné glacé with whipped cream, and three domestic wines.

When the tall Texan president rose to toast the tiny English princess, he offered advice to her young husband on how to keep a wife contented. "First, let her think she's having her way. Second, let her have it." By coincidence, it was also the Johnsons' thirty-first wedding anniversary, and the President gallantly hailed Lady Bird as "the most wonderful woman in the world." After the President's final toast to Queen Elizabeth II, the Johnsons and their royal guests led the way down the red-carpeted Cross Hall to the East Room. The great formal room had been transformed into an elegant cabaret with small tables circling the dance floor, each with a flickering candle in a hurricane lamp surrounded with fresh flowers. Peter Duchin's orchestra swung into "Everything's Coming Up Roses," but as the papers did not fail to report the next day, much of the evening's music was of the discothèque variety and Lord Snowdon proved very adept at the frug. The President, who was recuperating from surgery, confined himself to a sedate fox trot. And everyone wanted to dance with Princess Meg. Everyone included many of the most distinguished names in Washington and in American public life and society, but—unlike

The Diplomatic Reception Room

A bowl of white stock, yellow and bronze daisy and cushion chrys-anthemums, and bronze Duchess spoon chrysanthemums—in the Diplomatic Reception Room on the lower floor through which guests entered the White House.

Franklin D. Roosevelt and Dwight D. Eisenhower, who had invited only the highest-ranking dignitaries and social elite to their dinners for British royalty—the Johnsons had also extended invitations to numerous members of the White House staff.

The cabaret-style dance for Princess Margaret proved to be much livelier entertainment than the traditional after-dinner musicales that had greeted her parents and sister. In fact, the orchestra had to play "Good Night Ladies" twice before this enchanted evening drew to a close at 2 A.M., and the convalescing President and his Lady stayed until the end.

The East Room

On the Steinway grand piano at one end of the East Room, white snapdragons, yellow and white daisy and anemone chrysanthemums, large bronze disbud chrysanthemums, and yellow roses—in a vermeil bowl. The gold draperies have since been replaced by new ones ordered during the Kennedy restoration but not yet installed at this date.

The Second-Floor Oval Sitting Room

This is a view of the second-floor oval room, or family sitting room, as it appeared the night of the dinner dance. Painted yellow during the Kennedy restoration, as it had been during Dolley Madison's occupancy in 1809, the gracious chamber is furnished with Louis XVI chairs, tables, and commodes made in France and donated to the White House in 1962. They are similar to furnishings used by Thomas Jefferson at Monticello and at the White House. The room is directly over the oval Blue Room on the first floor. In the past it has often been used as the President's private study; the door at the right leads to the President's bedroom. Flanking the door are the United States and presidential flags, which are carried ahead when the First Family and guests of honor descend the grand staircase for a State dinner.

Blue delphinium and cornflowers, yellow, cream, and apricot gerbera daisies, white stock, miniature carnations, and candytuft, yellow calendula, and blue daisies—in one of the bamboo vermeil bowls donated by Mrs. Paul Mellon, on the table seen in the foreground, opposite. The pair of bronze candelabra belong to President and Mrs. Johnson.

The Second-Floor Oval Sitting Room

On one of a pair of matching marble-topped Louis XVI chests in the sitting room, large white and yellow disbud chrysanthemums, bronze Duchess spoon and cushion chrysanthemums, white daisy chrysanthemums, and podacarpus foliage—in one of a pair of vermeil mugs from the Biddle collection; the ornaments, vermeil sheafs of wheat from the same collection. Above, Paul Cézanne's "House on the Marne." Over the other chest (see page 36) with its matching bouquet, the painting is Cézanne's "The Forest."

The Cross Hall

In the background, the landing of the grand staircase that leads to the Entrance Foyer. Bronze small and Duchess spoon chrysanthemums, yellow and white daisy chrysanthemums, and white stock—in a Sèvres cachepot selected by Mrs. Theodore Roosevelt. The pier table, recently acquired as a gift, was made in France in 1810.

39

The Blue Room

The Entrance Foyer opens into the Cross Hall, where the central door is the entrance to the Blue Room. At either side, gold-fringed national and presidential flags on eagle-tipped standards; above, the golden official seal of the President of the United States. Framed in the doorway on the night of Princess Margaret's dinner dance, the bouquet above—Bermuda lilies, yellow and bronze pompon and daisy chrysanthemums, white stock, red anemones, and variegated red and white anemones—in a vermeil urn on the round center table.

Flowers in THE DIPLOMATIC RECEPTION ROOM

The most photographed spot in the Diplomatic Reception Room. Assorted anemones in many brilliant colors are perhaps the most effective of all the flowers used against the backdrop of the Niagara paddleboat scene on the antique painted wallpaper. (Luncheon for Chancellor Konrad Adenauer of Germany, November 21, 1961)

41

Bronze, yellow, red, and rust single and anemone chrysanthemums
with white sweet peas—in Chinese export bowl on a Baltimore- or
New England-made Federal table, circa 1800. Yellow-upholstered
sofa of the Federal period made in New York in the Hepplewhite
style; early-nineteenth-century card tables of New England origin
in the background at either side; and oval Aubusson-style rug made
especially for this room during the Eisenhower Administration. The
scenic wallpaper above the wainscoting, installed during the Kennedy
restoration, depicts here cadets and guests at West Point on the left
and a view of the Port of Boston on the right. (Judicial reception,
November 20, 1963, described on page 52)

The Diplomatic Reception Room

T HE USUAL ENTRANCE for guests arriving at the Executive Mansion is via the curving driveway to the South Portico and the Diplomatic Reception Room on the lower floor. The more formal entrance through the North Portico and the Entrance Foyer on the first floor is reserved for official greetings.

No other salon of the White House has accomplished such a successful social climb as the oval Diplomatic Reception Room, directly under the oval Blue Room on the first floor. Now a stately early-nineteenth-century parlor, it was once the boiler-furnace room. During the 1902 Theodore Roosevelt renovation, a sub-basement was excavated to house elsewhere such utilitarian necessities as the heating plant, and this area was made into a family sitting room opening out onto the garden. Franklin D. Roosevelt later selected the seldom-used room as the site for his famous Fireside Chats to the nation, and the setting was made more realistic when workmen managed to uncover a hearth that had been sealed off during previous alterations.

The National Society of Interior Designers made the room its special project in the second Eisenhower term, furnishing it with Federal tables and with an upholstered sofa and chairs made by New York and New England cabinet-makers of the late eighteenth and early nineteenth centuries. The fabrics, in shades of yellow, harmonize with the cream-colored Aubusson-style oval carpet into which are woven the seals of the fifty states.

Additional authentic American furnishings were donated during the Kennedy Administration, but the crowning glory is the beautiful antique wallpaper, "Scenic America," which was discovered in 1961 on the walls of a house in Thurmont, Maryland, that was about to be demolished. An enterprising young man bought it for only $500, carefully removed it, and brought it to Mrs. Kennedy, who persuaded the NSID to purchase it. The young man realized a handsome profit, but so also do all the White House visitors who see this delightful primitive panorama on the curving walls of the Diplomatic Reception Room. Made in France by Zuper & Company in Rixheim, Alsace, in 1834, the paper depicts such American wonders as Niagara Falls, Boston Harbor, Virginia's Natural Bridge, West Point, Lake George, and New York Bay. The gay coloring provides an unexcelled backdrop for bowls of fresh flowers. One particular spot has been repeatedly photographed. Near the exit to the hallway, a paddleboat steams fiercely through an expanse of brilliant blue water. The small bouquets placed by the lamp on the table below are always a blaze of color reflecting the medley of blues, greens, reds, and yellows in the panorama.

The Diplomatic Reception Room

Blue bachelor's-buttons, yellow and white single chrysanthemums and ranunculus, yellow miniature carnations, white roses, white buddleia, stevia, and geranium foliage—in Chinese export bowl against the Niagara background of the scenic wallpaper. Chinese lamp base, circa 1810; New England card table, circa 1800. (State dinner for Vice President Lyndon Johnson, Chief Justice Earl Warren, and Speaker of the House John W. McCormack, January 21, 1963)

44

White stock, yellow and bronze daisy and cushion chrysanthemums, and bronze Duchess spoon chrysanthemums against the same background. (Dinner dance for Princess Margaret and Lord Snowdon, November 17, 1965, described on page 33)

The Diplomatic Reception Room

Baby's-breath, wax-flower, single white chrysanthemums, yellow tulips, and yellow and salmon gerbera daisies—in small Chinese export bowl on the table in front of the yellow sofa. (State dinner for President and Señora Romulo Betancourt of Venezuela, February 19, 1963)

In the same bowl on the same table—yellow regal lilies, white marguerite daisies, gaillardia, coreopsis, and dusty miller foliage. (State luncheon for Dr. Carlos J. Arosemena Monroy, President of Ecuador, July 23, 1962)

Visitors leaving the Diplomatic Reception Room reach the Entrance Foyer on the first floor above by a nearby staircase and move from there to the Cross Hall, which stretches from the East Room to the State Dining Room, with the entrances to the Green, Blue, and Red rooms along its south wall in between. Opposite the Red Room stands a French Empire pier table brought to this country after Waterloo by Joseph Bonaparte, brother of Napoleon.

Bermuda lilies, maroon single and double stock, white stock and carnations, and Happiness red roses—in white ceramic basket on loan to the White House. (Luncheon for President Jorge Alessandri of Chile, December 11, 1962)

The Cross Hall

On the same Bonaparte pier table, Bermuda lilies, red and purple anemones, heather, white stock, blue iris, and pussy willow—in an antique grey wire basket. The portrait of George Washington is by Charles Peale Polk. (Reception for the Chiefs of Missions and State Department officials, February 21, 1963)

White lilies, stock, Majestic daisies, and peonies, white and yellow Killian daisies, yellow single chrysanthemums, lavender stock and sweetrocket, and pink weigela—in the same wire basket. The portrait of Washington is the more familiar one by Gilbert Stuart. (Luncheon for Senate wives, May 23, 1962)

Flowers in THE BLUE ROOM

Photographed shortly before the Kennedy restoration—yellow and white Peter-John chrysanthemums and single daisy chrysanthemums in a large blue urn presented to the White House by the French government; a metal tag (not seen) fastened to the plinth commemorates the inauguration of the Franco-American transatlantic cable on August 17, 1898, during the McKinley Administration. (State dinner for Prime Minister Jawaharlal Nehru of India, November 7, 1961, described on page 61)

Yellow single chrysanthemums and tritonia, white stock, yellow and white Killian daisies, and yellow Majestic daisies—in large vermeil (Biddle) bowl on center table covered with gold brocade. (Luncheon for Prince Souvanna Phouma, Prime Minister of the Royal Laotian Government, July 27, 1962)

The Blue Room

THE ARCHITECTURAL GEM of the White House is the oval Blue Room, where the President and First Lady customarily receive their guests. In President Monroe's day, when most of the furnishings had been created by French artisans, the chairs were upholstered in pinkish-red silk patterned with eagles framed in laurel wreaths. This same motif has been copied in today's brilliant blue upholstery installed during the Kennedy restoration. The room underwent several changes in color before President Martin Van Buren for the first time used a blue fabric there.

The classical revival furniture that President Madison had designed by Benjamin Henry Latrobe and executed by Baltimore cabinetmakers John and Hugh Findlay was destroyed when the British burned the White House in 1814. After the building's restoration, President Monroe ordered from the Parisian cabinetmaker, Bellangé, a suite for the Oval Room that included a sofa, pier table, two large mirrors, two upholstered *bergère* armchairs, eighteen *fauteuil* armchairs, eighteen side chairs, two screens, four stools, and six footstools, as well as curtains, a rug, and ornaments in glass, porcelain, and bronze-doré.

President James Buchanan replaced the fine French furniture with rococo Victorian pieces, including a circular, high-backed ottoman that dominated the center of the room. His ornate chairs and sofas, and the ottoman, were upholstered in cut velvet that heightened the busy effect of the patterned wallpaper and carpeting. President Chester A. Arthur redecorated the East, Red, and Green Rooms in similar Victorian style and further engaged Louis Comfort Tiffany to install a Tiffany-glass screen across the foyer entrance into the Cross Hall outside the Blue Room to provide privacy for the presidential family. Two administrations later, President Benjamin Harrison spent $45,370.75 for more redecoration. The ceiling of the Blue Room was done over in relief and fresco and the wainscot was trimmed with a frieze in relief. He had the gilding on the furniture repaired and purchased new draperies, laces, upholstery, and carpeting. The latter was even busier than its predecessor.

Much admired at the time, these Victorian furnishings endured through the McKinley Administration until, under the direction of President Theodore Roosevelt, the firm of McKim, Mead & White in 1902 designed furniture for the Blue Room in gilt and white. During the Kennedy restoration, sixty years later, these chairs were moved to the halls of the main floor, and four of Monroe's original Belangé chairs were recovered. The Monroe pier table, discarded during TR's day, was rediscovered in storage by Mrs. Kennedy and returned to its original position in the Blue Room, beneath a painting of George Washington. The walls were hung in a striped, two-toned, cream-colored satin. The woven design in the blue draperies is similar to the Monroe original of 1817. The Savonnerie rug and gilt-bronze and crystal chandelier are both early-nineteenth-century French. The graceful marble mantel of later vintage is the one designed by Stanford White in 1902, and it holds the famous gilded-bronze Minerva clock and candelabra that Monroe also purchased from France.

On November 20, 1963, President and Mrs. Kennedy held the annual Judicial reception in honor of members of the Supreme Court and officials of the Justice Department. Six hundred of the nation's leading federal jurists and attorneys, many of them President Kennedy's appointees, presented their gold-embossed admission cards at the entrance of the Diplomatic Reception Room. It was the cocktail hour and many of them came directly from their offices, meeting their wives there before going upstairs to the State rooms. More than one hundred others, for various reasons which they have since had cause to regret, were not able to attend.

The flower-room photographs taken on this day are not many but some are among the best in the entire collection. There may have been several reasons for this—it was the first official party of the 1963-64 social season and also Mrs. Kennedy's first appearance since the premature birth of her son, Patrick, three months before, as well as the thirty-eighth birthday of Attorney-General Robert F. Kennedy. But the pictures, noncommittally numbered and dated in their chronological place in the flower-room albums, have acquired their poignant significance for other reasons.

Supreme Court justices, members of the Cabinet, and their wives had gone directly upstairs to the family quarters, assembling in the yellow oval sitting room above the Blue Room. As the Marine band struck up "Hail to the Chief," they followed the President and Mrs. Kennedy down the curving main stairway to the Entrance Foyer where Mrs. Kennedy, looking radiantly beautiful in a raspberry-velvet suit, was greeted with admiring and sympathetic applause. The President, having decided to dispense with the formal Blue Room receiving line, plunged zestfully into the crowd and began shaking hands, circulating through the State rooms with Mrs. Kennedy following closely behind him.

52

The Blue Room

Photographed after the Kennedy restoration. On the velvet-covered center table, Scotch heather, white marguerite daisies, salmon, white, and pink gerbera daisies, blue iris, and large white, beige, salmon, and yellow single chrysanthemums—in a Biddle vermeil bowl. In the background, four of the original Monroe chairs ordered from France in 1817 and two reproductions; Empire torchère in bronze and brass at right; and portraits (left to right) of presidents Jackson, Monroe, and John Adams. French Savonnerie rug, circa 1820. (Judicial reception, November 20, 1963. Other pictures taken on this day are shown on pages 42, 68, and 73.)

53

The Robert Kennedys left early for the Attorney General's birthday celebration at Hickory Hill in Virginia, the same house where John and Jacqueline Kennedy had begun their married life before moving to Georgetown. The President and his wife stayed only twenty-two minutes at this, their last White House party. Without saying goodbye, they slipped quietly upstairs to prepare for their trip to Texas the following morning. Many of the guests stayed on for another gay hour or two, blissfully unaware of the President's approaching rendezvous with destiny in Dallas.

Blue and white agapanthus and white single chrysanthemums and Majestic daisies—in a Biddle vermeil bowl on the center table. (Luncheon for President-elect Guillermo Leon Valencia of Colombia, June 25, 1962)

The Blue Room

The Stanford White mantel in 1952, after the Truman restoration. Two bowls of daisies are wedged between the Monroe bronze-doré Minerva clock and candelabra. Mrs. Kennedy later discontinued the use of bouquets on mantels in the White House. The American-made furniture here was designed and acquired during the Theodore Roosevelt Administration and was removed to the halls during the Kennedy restoration. Firedog chenets of the Empire period, made in France.

54

The Blue Room

Yellow and white single chrysanthemums, white stock, apricot, white, and yellow single dahlias, and blue iris and delphinium—in a large Chinese export bowl. Ginori Italian ashtrays (contemporary); in the background, candelabrum and Minerva clock on the gilded Stanford White mantel. (Luncheon for President Sekou Touré of Guinea, October 10, 1962)

56

Flowers in THE RED ROOM

White miniature carnations, marguerite daisies, and annual and perennial baby's-breath, fuchsia sweet William, feverfew, and bachelor's-buttons, and maroon bachelor's-buttons—in an antique tole monteith on a rare nineteenth-century sofa table. The bust is of Henry Clay, who long hoped to live in the White House but three times tried, and failed, to be elected President of the United States. (Luncheon for Idaho editors and publishers, June 15, 1962)

Lavender and white daisy chrysanthemums, pink snapdragons and roses, lavender heather, and rubrum lilies—in a small vermeil monteith from the Biddle collection, placed on the same sofa table, attributed to the French cabinetmaker, Charles Honoré Lannuier, who worked in New York from 1803 to 1819. Lamp base is marble and gilt-bronze Empire urn, circa 1820. Many of the flower room's most charming small bouquets have been arranged for this particular spot in the Red Room. (Dinner dance for Princess Margaret and Lord Snowdon, November 17, 1965, described on page 33.)

The Red Room

T HE EXQUISITE RED ROOM, located between the Blue Room and the State Dining Room, today resembles an Empire parlor of the early nineteenth century. The first of the State chambers to be refurnished by the Fine Arts Commission during the Kennedy Administration, its walls are hung with a bright cerise silk fabric bordered in gold, woven after a French sample of the period and matched to a red-and-beige Savonnerie carpet on the floor. Above a large French desk with glittering ormolu mounts hangs a fascinating convex mirror, probably of the Jackson era, which was found in White House storage. Recently returned to the mansion and placed in the Red Room are two rosewood chairs of the Empire-Victorian transitional period, which had been used during the Lincoln Administration and later sold at public auction.

The Red Room was once the setting for a secret presidential inauguration. Inaugural Day fell on a Sunday in the year 1877 and, because the challenging of a one-vote victory in the Electoral College had plunged the nation into bitter political wrangling, President Grant took unusual precautions for an orderly succession of office. He invited President-elect and Mrs. Rutherford B. Hayes to dine at the White House on Saturday, March 3, 1887. The table in the State Dining Room was set for thirty-six guests, with a large bouquet of flowers at each place. A pink azalea ten feet high stood immediately behind Mrs. Hayes' chair, an arrangement that probably delighted flower-loving "Lemonade Lucy" Hayes more than the six wine glasses at each place setting.

Promptly at midnight President Grant signaled to Hayes, Chief Justice Morrison R. Waite, and Secretary of State Hamilton Fish to follow him into the Red Room. There, unknown to most of the guests, the Chief Justice administered the presidential oath to Hayes, with Fish as the only witness. A day and a half later, on a Monday, the oath of office was repeated in a public ceremony at the Capitol.

Because of its warmth and homelike atmosphere, President Kennedy customarily used the Red Room to receive the credentials of newly arrived ambassadors from foreign nations. This was regarded as the music room throughout much of the nineteenth century and today it still houses a small Empire music stand on which has been placed the sheet music for "Lafayette's March," written to honor the Marquis on his famous return visit, in 1825, to the America he had helped so much to make a nation.

The Red Room

The Red Room with the plain silk walls of the Kennedy restoration. On the Monroe mantel, an eighteenth-century French musical clock presented by President Vincent Auriol of France in 1952; above it, "The Last of the Mohicans" painted in 1857 by Asher B. Durand of the Hudson River school. Andirons, or chenets, are French gilt bronze. The graceful Empire sofa with gilded dolphin feet is upholstered in cerise and gold. Far right, portrait (1919) of Woodrow Wilson by the English painter Sir William Orpen.

All-white arrangements are particularly effective in this room. Here, an autumn bouquet of white stock and daisy and disbud chrysanthemums—in Biddle vermeil urn on a Federal card table. American Empire chair at left; portrait of William Henry Harrison, 1879, by Eliphalet Andrews, after an earlier James Beard painting.

State dinner for Prime Minister Jawaharlal Nehru of India, November 7, 1961. Mr. Nehru was accompanied by his daughter, Mrs. Indira Gandhi, who within a few years would herself become Prime Minister. The State dinner on this evening was one of the smallest and most elegant of the Kennedy Administration. As Mr. Nehru had requested a "private" visit to this country, the list of guests was limited to thirty. Among them were Princess Lee Radziwill, the First Lady's sister, who later accompanied Mrs. Kennedy on a visit to India and Pakistan, and Vice President Johnson, Secretary of State Dean Rusk, the late Ambassador to the United Nations Adlai Stevenson, and two former ambassadors to India, Ellsworth Bunker and Senator John Sherman Cooper. Among all the flowers on display that evening, one blossom had a traditional importance of its own—the single fresh rose invariably worn by the Indian Prime Minister.

The Red Room

The winged-sphinx support of the Lannuier sofa table shows below an arrangement of white marguerite daisies, sweet peas, freesia, and baby's-breath—again in the antique tole monteith. In back, a bouillotte lamp of the French Empire period, a gift to the White House during the Kennedy Administration. (Reception for representatives of the Alliance for Progress, March 13, 1962)

On the sofa table, the full height of the bouillotte lamp behind an all-white arrangement of miniature carnations, marguerite daisies, and ranunculus, with dusty miller foliage —in the tole monteith. (Dinner for His Excellency Luis Muñoz Marin, Governor of Puerto Rico, November 13, 1961, followed by the famous performance of the Spanish cellist, Pablo Casals, described on page 80)

The Red Room

All-white spring bouquet—tulips, Bermuda lilies, chrysanthemums, Majestic, Killian, and marguerite daisies, and cherry blossoms—in vermeil Biddle urn between a pair of vermeil ornaments. The walls are covered with the plain silk bordered by a formal scroll design in gold woven for the Kennedy restoration. The American Empire card table is one of a pair, also attributed to Charles Honoré Lannuier. American Empire chair is one of a very fine pair given by a private donor. The Gilbert Stuart portrait, then on loan, is no longer in the White House. (Luncheon for President Joao Goulart of Brazil, April 3, 1962)

64

Flowers in THE GREEN ROOM

Lavender and pink stock, yellow and brown oncidium orchids, white and yellow single chrysanthemums and Killian daisies, white peonies, lavender sweetrocket, and yellow iris—in a late-eighteenth-century Chinese export bowl acquired during the Hoover Administration, on one of the Federal card tables. Above, Cézanne's "The Forest," willed to the White House by a private donor; this painting was later moved to the oval sitting room on the second floor. The wall hanging is that used before the Kennedy restoration. (Luncheon for Senate wives, May 23, 1962)

The Green Room in 1966. Over the flowers on the matched pair of Federal card tables at either side of the doorway are, left, Claude Monet's "Morning on the Seine" (shown on page 29) donated in memory of President Kennedy and, to the right, James Whistler's "London Nocturne." The portraits are of John James Audubon, Angelica Van Buren (President Van Buren's daughter-in-law and his official hostess at the White House) and, over the mantel, Benjamin Franklin.

The Green Room

T HE GREEN ROOM is the counterpart, to the east of the Blue Room, of the Red Room to the west. It was originally intended by Thomas Jefferson and English architect Benjamin Henry Latrobe as a Common Dining Room. But it has consistently been used as a parlor and nowadays also serves as an elegant passageway for the receiving line that wends its way from the East Room to the Blue Room when the President and First Lady greet their guests there at large receptions.

Like its neighboring salons, the Green Room has undergone frequent refurbishings as fashions changed. With the Kennedy restoration, it was refurnished in the graceful Federal style of 1800. The lovely marble Empire mantel is one of the two ordered from France by President Monroe in 1817 for the State Dining Room, where they remained until Theodore Roosevelt reinstalled them in the Green and Red rooms. On the Green Room mantel are the famed Hannibal bronze-doré clock and vases purchased by Monroe from France. The wall hangings since the Kennedy restoration are of moss-green watered silk, and the late-eighteenth-century English Axminster carpet is in the Adam style.

Some of the recently acquired antiques in the Green Room are an American-made secretary, two Martha Washington armchairs, and a French Louis XVI armchair believed to have been used by George Washington in the Executive Mansion when the seat of government was in Philadelphia. The room also houses a matched pair of New England Federal card tables (*circa* 1800) donated by the Crowninshield family, flanked by four lattice-back chairs attributed to the renowned woodcarver, Samuel McIntire, of Salem, Massachusetts, and a mahogany sofa banded with satinwood that once belonged to Daniel Webster. In front of the sofa is a round Baltimore Federal table, made in about 1805, on which a bowl of flowers used to be placed. Today, it holds a large Sheffield coffee urn that originally belonged to President John Adams. In his inventory of 1826 he referred to it as "one of my most prized possessions." A medallion on one side is engraved with both his and his wife's initials, "JAA." Mr. Mark Bortman, a Bostonian, purchased it from the Adams family in the late 1940s. Mr. Bortman has taken a lively interest in the People-to-People program and was concerned in the famous visit to America, by invitation of Vice President Johnson, of a Pakistani camel driver. After Mr. Johnson became President, Mr. Bortman donated the precious urn to the White House.

67

*Yellow and white marguerite daisies and blue iris in an antique
Chinese export bowl. Federal Baltimore table, circa 1805, in front of
Daniel Webster's New England Sheraton sofa, of the same period.
Since the Johnson Administration, the Sheffield coffee urn that
belonged to President John Adams is usually placed here instead of
flowers. (Judicial reception, November 20, 1963, described on page
52)*

The Green Room

Forsythia, orange, yellow, and white gerbera daisies, orange freesia and ranunculus, and ornamental oranges—in a large Chinese export bowl on one of the Crowninshield card tables. Lattice-back chair to the left attributed to Samuel McIntire. (Luncheon for President Sylvanus E. Olympio of Togo, March 20, 1962)

The Green Room

White stock and yellow anemone and bronze single chrysanthemums in a vermeil tureen from the Biddle collection that is particularly good for a low arrangement under a painting—again on one of the pair of Federal card tables. (Luncheon for the U.S.-Japanese Committee on Trade and Economic Affairs, December 3, 1962, attended by five members of President Kennedy's Cabinet and numerous high-ranking Japanese officials, including the Foreign Minister and Finance Minister)

70

Completely ingenuous, a bunch of crisp white marguerite daisies in a Chinese export mug—on a secretary made in about 1795 by Joseph Burgess of Baltimore. The exquisite green-glass and gilt-bronze inkwell dates from the early nineteenth century and is probably of French origin. (Luncheon for President Sekou Touré of Guinea, October 10, 1962)

The Green Room

White peonies, Majestic and marguerite daisies, white and lavender sweetrocket, rubrum lilies, and lavender double stock—again in the Biddle vermeil tureen. In the background, the green watered-silk wall hanging, banded with narrow braid, of the Kennedy restoration. (Luncheon for Senate wives, May 15, 1963)

Flowers in THE EAST ROOM

French heather, stevia, yellow, white, beige, salmon, rust, bronze, and red single chrysanthemums, and white anemone and Duchess spoon chrysanthemums—in eighteenth-century Roman marble urn selected by Mrs. Theodore Roosevelt. Directly opposite the entrance from the Cross Hall, the massive bouquet in front of the richly curtained window is the visitor's first glimpse of the gold-and-white East Room. Stanford White bench; stands on either side for ashtrays and glasses from a set made in the White House carpentry shop. The gold draperies have since been changed. (Judicial reception, November 20, 1963, described on page 52.)

White carnations, apple blossoms, wild-cherry blossoms, cream and red tulips, white, yellow, and orange gerbera daisies, and eucalyptus foliage—in a pair of Sèvres cachepots also selected by Mrs. Theodore Roosevelt in 1902. The pier tables and the bench in front of the window were designed by Stanford White. The massive Steinway piano with golden eagle supports was donated to the White House during Franklin D. Roosevelt's second term. (Luncheon for Prime Minister and Mrs. Constantinos Caramanlis of Greece, April 17, 1961)

Known as the Public Audience Chamber in Thomas Jefferson's day, the East Room is the largest and most formal in the White House. In the years since Mrs. John (Abigail) Adams used its unfinished expanse as a place to hang her laundry, it has experienced almost as many ups and downs as our two political parties. Dolley Madison held public audience here every Wednesday evening, and from two to three hundred Washingtonians thronged the East Room on each occasion. On August 24, 1814, while British soldiers stormed the very doors of Washington, Dolley valiantly waited to flee until Gilbert Stuart's portrait of George Washington could be removed from its heavy frame and sent into hiding. All that was left of the White House after that night of horror was the blackened shell, for the Redcoats put a torch to it.

The nation promptly began the rebuilding of the mansion, but it was so sparsely furnished that, before President James Monroe could hold a New Year's reception there in 1818, he agreed to sell his own fine furniture to the government at bargain prices. This he had purchased, while living in Paris, from nobility impoverished by the French Revolution. Thanks to his cosmopolitan tastes, the government also made other purchases of handsome French table services and ornamental pieces that still survive today and are the most valuable in the White House collection.

During Monroe's Administration, the East Room was furnished with four sofas and twenty-four chairs. These survived until the Jackson Inauguration, when rustic celebrants stormed into the White House, stood in their muddy boots on the delicate furniture, cut swatches from the draperies, trampled food into the carpeting, and created such a shambles that Old Hickory had to escape through a window to a nearby hotel for the night. Congress fortunately came to the rescue, and the Squire of the Hermitage used a liberal appropriation to paper the East Room in "a fine lemon color," to install four black marble mantels under four great mirrors, and to purchase three gilt and cut-glass chandeliers. Under each chandelier he placed a round table topped with an Italian black and gold marble slab, and the same marble was used on the new side tables. The Monroe furniture was restuffed and re-covered and nearly five hundred yards of fine Brussels carpet were laid on the refinished floors. The East Room refurbishing also included four sets of fireplace brasses and twenty spittoons. President Jackson displayed the dazzling new effect at a reception for a thousand guests, where the *pièces de résistance* at the lavish buffet were two "monster salmon in waves of meat jelly" at either end of a horseshoe table in the State Dining Room.

The East Room again fell into dismal disrepair after the assassination of Abraham Lincoln. His grieving widow remained closeted in her room upstairs and, during the several months before she could be gently persuaded to vacate the White House, the public rooms were so disgracefully looted that the incoming Andrew Johnsons had to use fresh bouquets at strategic points to hide the holes, stains, and scuff marks. The Johnson women performed much of the scrubbing and renovation themselves. Congress helped with funds for redecoration, but the mansion had barely been returned to a semblance of order when a defective flue caused a damaging fire. The flames also raced through the conservatory built by President Buchanan and destroyed a third of its plants, including a rare sago palm that had been imported by George Washington.

Until General Ulysses S. Grant moved to the White House in 1869, the East Room had been notable for its classic simplicity, its fluted pilasters and cornices decorated with Greek palmettes. Tastes decidedly changed during the Victorian era, however, and Grant ordered the ceiling and cornices heavily overlaid with furbelows. The chaste Georgian effect vanished beneath the plush cloaking, and one critic aptly grumbled that it resembled the main saloon of a Long Island steamer. President Chester A. Arthur added still more suffocating embellishments to this steamboat-palace décor, and not until Theodore Roosevelt directed his complete renovation of the mansion in 1902 did the elegant simplicity of the East Room ceiling and walls again emerge.

Gold and white have been colors often used in this room, though Franklin Roosevelt substituted red draperies and carpeting, personally selecting the color from a variety of swatches. The beautiful chamber reverted to gold with the 1948-52 Truman reconstruction.

The East Room

White and lavender stock, yellow and orange gerbera daisies, forsythia, white and yellow carnations, and eucalyptus foliage—one of another pair of arrangements in the Sèvres cachepots, on one of the pair of pier tables designed by Stanford White for the East Room. (Reception for Chiefs of Missions and their wives, February 8, 1961)

76

The East Room

The East Room as it appeared during the McKinley Administration. The "steamboat-palace" Victorian décor dated from the Grant renovation of 1873 and the upholstering from the Arthur refurbishing of 1882. In the high fashion of the era, vines were twined around the gilded pillars and chandeliers, and potted plants and palms abounded.

78

The classic simplicity of the East Room was first restored by Theodore Roosevelt. The Stanford White benches designed for it are today upholstered in gold; the Roosevelt chandeliers have been shortened. The mantels were installed during the Truman reconstruction. New gold silk damask draperies, ordered for the Kennedy restoration, were installed during the Johnson Administration. Woven to order in France, the intricate design of the damask runs without repetition for sixteen feet, the length of each curtain. The tasseled swag valences used before have been eliminated and the curtains hang simply in straight folds, from gilt cornices that were installed in 1902. In the distance, Steinway grand piano with golden eagle supports; to the right, full-length portraits of George and Martha Washington.

After formal dinners, the East Room is frequently transformed into a luxurious auditorium where performances by celebrated artists are held. Surely one of the most brilliant of such occasions was the appearance of the 85-year-old Spanish cellist, Pablo Casals, following a State dinner for the Governor of Puerto Rico, Luis Muñoz Marin, on November 13, 1961. It was an evening that will long be remembered, too, as the epitome of the "style" of the Kennedy Administration. Maestro Casals, for many years in self-imposed exile in Puerto Rico because of his opposition to Generalissimo Franco's rightist regime in Spain, played at the White House that night for the first time in fifty-seven years. The only guest who had also been present at his previous White House appearance was "Princess" Alice Roosevelt Longworth, who had heard him play in 1904 for her father, President Theodore Roosevelt. Among other guests were many of today's most distinguished men of music—Aaron Copland, Howard Hanson, Virgil Thomson, Leopold Stokowski, William Schuman, Eugene Ormandy, Leonard Bernstein, Gian Carlo Menotti. Casals played Schumann's *Adagio* and *Allegro* and was afterwards accompanied by Pianist Mieczyslaw Horszowski and Violinist Alexander Schneider in Mendelssohn's *Trio in D Minor*. It was music such as may never have been excelled in the White House.

Looking down upon this most exceptional of cultural events were the two massive full-length portraits that have long dominated the beautiful East Room: an oil of Martha Washington, painted by Eliphalet Andrews in the late nineteenth century from earlier pictures, and Stuart's George Washington which Dolley Madison rescued from the British soldiers.

The East Room

Lavender campanula and larkspur, blue delphinium, heliopsis, white Killian daisies, Majestic daisies, delphinium, and annual baby's-breath—in the Roman marble urn. (Luncheon for Archbishop Makarios III of Cyprus, June 5, 1962)

Flowers in THE STATE DINING ROOM

Yellow and white tulips and freesia, orange and lavender freesia, blue iris, yellow and orange Mid-Century lilies, leucocoryne, baby's-breath, lavender anemones, paperwhite narcissus, yellow and cream narcissus, tristus, and blue daisies—in Biddle vermeil tureen. Monroe French surtout-de-table, Kennedy crystal, blue and gold Truman china, Monroe flatware, Biddle vermeil nut dish.

81

The picture on the preceding page was taken before the State luncheon for the King of Laos, Sri Savang Vatthana, and his son, Prince Sourya Vong Savang, on February 25, 1963. Although Mrs. Kennedy favored small round tables for ten, for this stag occasion the President used a U-shaped table, with Vice President Johnson seated here, opposite him, on the inner loop of the horseshoe. The menu: Bouchée of lobster américaine, filet mignon béarnaise, string beans aux amandes, potatoes Champs Elysées, bombe glacée Virginie and petits-fours.

Red sweet William, maroon bachelor's-buttons, and white feverfew—in Biddle vermeil tureen, on console designed by Stanford White in 1902. (Luncheon for Minister of Foreign Affairs Paul-Henri Spaak of Belgium, June 9, 1962)

82

The State Dining Room

THE STATE DINING ROOM today is nearly double its original size. Throughout the nineteenth century, the so-called Public Dining Room proved adequate except at large State dinners, when long tables had to be set up in the drafty corridor leading to the Entrance Foyer. During the Theodore Roosevelt renovation, the main staircase separating the dining room from a smaller chamber that had originally been intended as a bedroom was removed. By incorporating the stair well and a portion of the hallway, the spacious proportions of the present-day State Dining Room were happily achieved. The room was paneled in carved natural oak, with Corinthian pilasters and a frieze of carved sheaves and festoons under the classic cornice. The two delicate Monroe mantels were removed to the Green and Red rooms, and a massive mantel with carved buffalo heads was centered on the west wall. High-backed chairs in Queen Anne style, still used today, were ordered through McKim, Mead & White, and Stanford White also designed for this room three marble-topped consoles supported by eagles.

During the Truman reconstruction, the dark wall paneling was taken down, later carefully reinstalled and painted a soft green. A simple molding of light verd antique Vermont marble was substituted for Teddy Roosevelt's mantel. Mrs. Kennedy subsequently changed the room's décor to off-white, gilded the Roosevelt chandelier and wall sconces, and gave several coats of off-white paint to Stanford White's consoles. Since the original buffalo mantel had by then been incorporated into the Truman Library at Independence, Missouri, the Kennedys had a replica made and removed the Vermont-marble one.

The most famous and magnificent of the Monroe French bronzes is the mirror-plateau centerpiece, or *surtout-de-table,* used in this room on State occasions. Also in the White House collection are Monroe bronze-doré and vermeil urns, baskets, and candelabra, vermeil compotes and tureens from the Margaret Biddle collection, and, recently donated by Mrs. Paul Mellon, a set of Tiffany vermeil bowls in bamboo design—altogether a remarkable assortment of containers for flowers in the State Dining Room.

State dinners and other entertainment at the White House have varied markedly in style, as much according to the temperaments and prejudices of the presidents and their first ladies as to the fashion of the day. Some first families

The State Dining Room . . .

. . . as it appeared during the Eisenhower Administration for a State
dinner honoring the Cabinet, on December 1, 1954. The walls were
a soft green. The Monroe surtout-de-table and vases the length of
the E-shaped table held a profusion of Mrs. Eisenhower's favorite
pink carnations flown from her native Denver; smilax festooned the
table and fireplace molding. Monroe candelabra and flatware, Truman
china, Franklin D. Roosevelt crystal, Biddle vermeil nut dishes. The
George Inness landscape above the mantel was later removed to the
National Gallery of Art.

have been gastronomically minded, others not, but none surpassed in sheer size the gargantuan feasts dispensed by President and Mrs. Ulysses S. Grant. The belt-tightening Civil War was over when the hero of Appomattox moved to the White House in 1869, and dieting had not yet come into vogue. For one Grant State dinner, twenty-four courses were served. At the halfway mark, the guests arose, strolled around the room to stretch their legs and helped themselves to Roman fruit punch laced with rum. Dozens of yards of vines intertwined with flowers decorated the banquet table in swag arrangement, and individual nosegays were placed at each lady's plate and boutonnières at the gentlemen's.

If we can believe the society writers of the day, even this extravaganza was topped by the wedding, in 1874, of the Grants' eighteen-year-old daughter, Nellie, to Algernon Charles Frederick Sartoris, handsome blond nephew of the actress Fanny Kemble. Nellie Grant pledged her troth in the East Room under a great floral wedding bell suspended from a floral arch that displayed the floral monograms of bride and groom. The guests then retired to the State Dining Room "wherein was spread a table that has probably never been excelled in this country for richness, artistic skill, or systematic arrangement." The "pearly-white, flower-crowned bridal cake extended a decoration of natural flowers," and miniature flags that adorned the table carried such legends as "Success to the President," "Success to the Army," and "Hail Columbia." Sad to tell, Nellie's marriage lasted but a few years.

Despite his lavish entertainment, the Civil War general may have been upstaged in the privacy of his own dining room. One reporter recorded that when the family was alone, Colonel Frederick Dent, an unreconstructed Southern Democrat who violently disagreed with his presidential son-in-law's political views, used to occupy the head of the table, with the President seated at his left and Mrs. Grant at his right. The President's father, Jesse Grant, who also spent considerable time at the White House, carried on a running battle with Colonel Dent.

The Hayes Administration had a well-known quirk in matters of entertaining. President and Mrs. Rutherford B. Hayes permitted wine to be served at a State dinner honoring the Russian Grand Dukes Alexis and Constantin, but thereafter they banned all alcoholic beverages from the White House, thus earning Mrs. Hayes the unofficial title of "Lemonade Lucy." However, this did not discourage Washingtonians from swarming to her receptions, which were held nightly and were open to the public.

Despite the Gay Nineties, the McKinley Administration was not particularly noted for its gaiety. The Teddy Roosevelt years that followed brought not only one of the most important renovations in the history of the White House but also a series of spectacular social events. There was the huge wedding of the President's daughter, "Princess" Alice, to Congressman Nicholas Longworth of Ohio, and the debutante ball in honor of her half-sister, Ethel, for which the State Dining Room was cleared for dancing and dinner was served on the lower floor. A painting commemorating TR's stag dinner party for Prince Henry of Germany, brother of the Kaiser, in February of 1902, shows that the style of the day in floral decoration still included a smothering profusion of flowers on the dinner table as well as potted palms and garlands twined about columns and bordering the paneling. In some contradiction to the elegance that Theodore Roosevelt gave to the State Dining Room were the mounted heads of hartebeests and antelopes he had shot and which he had hung on the walls.

William Howard Taft, too, set a considerable social pace, holding during the first two months of his term of office six State dinners, two garden parties, and innumerable lesser functions. State dinners were discontinued during the World War I years of the Wilson Administration and, when they were resumed, Prohibition barred once again the serving of wines at the White House, though President Harding reportedly poured hard liquor for himself and his friends upstairs.

Not until the frugal Calvin Coolidge took office did Congress for the first time vote an official-entertainment fund for presidents. Mr. Coolidge inaugurated a series of breakfasts for members of Congress in the State Dining Room. He also provided one of the quainter stories associated with this room. Toward the end of a State dinner, formally attired guests tried not to stare as the President removed the saucer from under his cup and poured cream into it. Puzzled but eager to do the right thing, many of them unwisely did the same. The President, however, set the saucer on the floor and called the cat.

The sophisticated, well-traveled Herbert Hoovers were as lavish in their entertaining as the Coolidges had been penny-pinching, and the chief usher, who had seen numerous administrations come and go, later reported that the Hoovers provided "the best table that was ever set in the White House." Eleanor Roosevelt was more interested in her many activities for social reform than she was in elegant cuisine. On Sunday evenings, she often sat at the dinner table with a silver chafing dish beside her, merrily scrambling eggs for family and guests. However, it was during the Franklin D. Roosevelt era that a much-needed modern kitchen was installed in the basement of the aging mansion.

During World War II, foreign dignitaries came in droves to the White House and Winston Churchill flew to Washington on several historic occasions. But perhaps the most memorable event of official hospitality in the Roosevelt years

The State Dining Room . . .

. . . after the Kennedy restoration. The room is now off-white and gold, and a replica of Theodore Roosevelt's buffalo mantel has been installed. A portrait of Abraham Lincoln by George P. A. Healy hangs above it. On the long head table and on the round tables for ten, bouquets in vermeil bamboo-design bowls made by Tiffany's and donated to the White House by Mrs. Paul Mellon. The flowers were gaillardia, coreopsis, baby's-breath; white, fuchsia, and lavender sweet William; white, fuchsia, and beige miniature carnations; white Shasta daisies; yellow, white, and blue iris. The gilt chairs, copies of a set owned by the Mellons, were purchased during the Kennedy Administration. Monroe flatware, Truman china, and Kennedy crystal. (State dinner for Dr. Sarvepalli Radhakrishnan, President of India, June 3, 1963)

The State Dining Room

A single low bouquet of lily-of-the-valley, tuberoses, blue delphinium, miniature white, yellow, lavender, and maroon carnations, lavender cosmos, yellow and white marguerite daisies and single chrysanthemums—in Monroe bronze-doré basket simply centered on three sections of the Monroe mirror-plateau centerpiece. Four additional sections can stretch the centerpiece to a length of thirteen and a half feet. Truman china, Kennedy crystal, Monroe flatware. State dinner for Emperor Haile Selassie of Ethiopia, October 1, 1963. The setting in the foreground was that of the President's mother, Mrs. Joseph P. Kennedy. Directly opposite, the President's chair, the Emperor's next to it. In the background, the replica of the Theodore Roosevelt buffalo mantel, engraved with a passage from a letter written by President John Adams: "I pray Heaven to bestow the best of blessings on this house and all that shall hereafter inhabit it. May none but honest and wise men ever rule under this roof."

was in the last months of peace in Europe—the dinner in honor of King George VI of England and Queen Elizabeth, on June 8, 1939. The regilded *surtout-de-table* at the head of the U-shaped table was massed with small purple-tipped white orchids, lilies-of-the-valley, and maidenhair fern. Tall white tapers gleamed in the Monroe candelabra, and gold flatware shone on the white damask cloth beside new Lenox china embossed with the Roosevelt family crest. A generation later, when a war had been fought and won, a setting of similar elegance was once again devised for the Eisenhower State dinner honoring young Queen Elizabeth II, who had succeeded her father to the throne, and Prince Philip. Biddle vermeil tureens and compotes, as well as the priceless Monroe bronze-doré centerpiece and baskets, held pyramids of carnations and purple orchids. At least twenty-five orchids were used in each of the thirty bouquets along the expanse of the E-shaped table, which was covered with white damask draped with garlands of smilax.

The Trumans resumed the official social schedule after World War II, but only briefly at the White House. Vibrating floors and ominously tinkling chandeliers provoked the inspection that disclosed the historic mansion was in danger of collapse. The First Family moved across the street to Blair House, to remain there for nearly four years while the Truman reconstruction was to be under way. The next State dinner in the State Dining Room, with the White House barely ready again to receive guests, was for Queen Juliana of the Netherlands and Prince Bernhard in 1952.

The traditional U-shaped table in the State Dining Room was often E-shaped during the Eisenhower Administration. Flowers, such as Mamie Eisenhower's favorite pink carnations flown from her native Denver, were arranged handsomely in traditional banquet-table style. The Kennedys, after briefly reverting to the U-shape, soon discarded this formality in favor of separate round tables for ten and a relatively small oblong head table. At unusually large State dinners, President Kennedy headed the official table and Jacqueline Kennedy presided at one of the round tables in the Blue Room which held the overflow. On these smaller tables—which served as conversational circles that no banquet table could provide—Mrs. Kennedy's multicolored bouquets of seasonal flowers were often arranged in the Mellon bamboo vermeil bowls. A hostess with the courage of her convictions, Mrs. Kennedy engaged a noted French chef, served excellent French wines, and had the formal menus placed at each setting written in French. She dared to be an innovator, to substitute ballet, Shakespearean readings, and chamber music for the light entertainment of previous times. The young President, though more of a steak-and-potatoes man, delighted in his beautiful wife's knowledgeable performance as the first hostess in the land, and the brilliance of Kennedy State dinners and social events became legendary overnight.

The State Dining Room

Yellow and white tulips and freesia, orange and lavender freesia, blue iris, leucocoryne, baby's-breath, lavender anemones, paperwhite narcissus, yellow and cream narcissus, venidium, and blue daisies—in one of the set of vermeil bamboo bowls.

90

Vice President and Mrs. Johnson were usually present at Kennedy functions ranging from State dinners to the unofficial small dances for friends and relatives. The breezy Texans, accustomed to the informality of the Southwest, liked the more relaxed atmosphere. Details such as the State Dining Room round tables and the varied unconventional bouquets from the flower room are still Mrs. Johnson's preference and her own ideas in the same vein have been both delightful and interesting. She has taken particular note of the collection of presidential china, samples of which are on display in the China Room on the lower floor, but which otherwise languishes in storage closets because few of the sets are now complete enough to be used for large gatherings. Mrs. Johnson first put the collection to use in the State Dining Room at her spring, 1964, luncheon for Senate wives. Lady Bird Johnson saw, too, the possibility of using the East and West Terraces—actually the roofs of the pavilions that connect the mansion with the two office wings—and has given dinner dances there under the summertime moon, with potted plants screening the terraces from busy Pennsylvania Avenue.

The most talked of party of the Johnson Administration surely is the dinner dance given in honor of Princess Margaret and Lord Snowdon in the fall of

Yellow and white tulips and freesia, blue iris, orange and yellow Mid-Century lilies, leucocoryne, baby's breath, paper-white narcissus, tristus, and blue daisies—in a Monroe vermeil basket urn. Both pictures, State luncheon for the King of Laos, February 25, 1963. Taken before the banquet table was set, this picture shows in the background a fragment of the gold embroidery on the cloth donated to the White House by the firm of Porthault, designed to be used with the collections of bronze-doré and vermeil accessories.

1965. Pictures of the State Dining Room taken that day (pages 25, 26, and 27), when the tables had been set and the flowers put in place, show it at its most resplendent, a room that today has all the dignity Theodore Roosevelt intended for it and an elegant charm it has sometimes lacked in the past.

The State Dining Room

White carnations and miniature carnations, yellow carnations, yellow and bronze daisy chrysanthemums, yellow marguerite daisies and calendula, and sumac foliage—in Monroe bronze-doré basket on the great surtout-de-table. Truman china, Kennedy crystal, Monroe flatware, Biddle vermeil nut dish. Opposite: The same flowers massed in a Biddle vermeil compote.

Dinner for former President Harry S Truman and Mrs. Truman, November 1, 1961. This was a nostalgic evening for the peppery former President, who had not entered the Executive Mansion during the Eisenhower Administration. To toast their former chief, President Kennedy invited officials who had worked with Mr. Truman during his administration, including many members of the Truman Cabinet, and Vice President and Mrs. Johnson, Margaret Truman and her husband Clifton Daniel, and close friends. Although he may not have translated all the French on the menu card, Mr. Truman was reported to have thoroughly enjoyed the cuisine, which consisted of mousse de crabe, grouse à l'américaine, riz sauvage nature, haricots verts au beurre, céleri braisé, salade mimosa, ananas voilé Judith and petits-fours. The wines were Puligny-Montrachet Les Pucelles 1958, Château Gruaud-Larose 1955, and Cuvée Dom Perignon Brut 1952.

93

The State Dining Room

Yellow, red, and orange single and pompon dahlias, white marguerite daisies and stock, yellow and bronze single daisy chrysanthemums, and buddleia—in a silver bowl on a silver plateau centerpiece with eagle motif designed by William Forbes of New York City, circa 1810. Franklin D. Roosevelt china, Kennedy crystal. (Luncheon for Foreign Ministers of Latin America, October 2, 1962)

An entirely different, stylized topiary arrangement of yellow and white carnations, red and yellow nasturtiums, narcissus, and magnolia leaves—in the same vermeil compote seen on the previous page. Truman china, Franklin Roosevelt crystal. (Luncheon for Premier Constantine Karamanlis of Greece and Mrs. Karamanlis, April 17, 1961)

The Lincoln China. Anemones, yellow and white marguerite daisies, lily-of-the-valley, baby's-breath, beige miniature carnations, and white ranunculus—in James Polk French porcelain high fruit bowl. Similar bouquets were used on all the tables at this luncheon for Senate wives.

Luncheon for Senate wives, May 6, 1964. Lady Bird Johnson had been a Senate wife for so many years before her husband became President that she knew intimately all the members of the club that is officially named the Senate Ladies' Red Cross Group. Wearing white uniform and cap veil, she had participated in countless Tuesday sessions, bringing her own lunch and wrapping bandages for military hospitals. While Lyndon Johnson was Vice President, she was the group's presiding officer.

As a consequence, her heart was in her work as she planned "a very special treat" for the Senate wives at the White House Luncheon in their honor when she became First Lady. It had to be different, and it was. A glorious sight awaited the 110 senatorial wives and widows when they walked into the State Dining Room that lovely spring day. For the first time in history, a choice selection of the china patterns designed for various presidents of the United States were in simultaneous use. Each round table for ten was set with a different service, and even George Washington's china was there, the colors of the floral border, banded in gold, picked up by the fresh flowers of the centerpiece. All the bouquets were arranged in historic compotes and fruit bowls.

The ladies lunched on prosciutto and melon, suprême of chicken Maryland, purée favorite, and fresh fruit au Cointreau. The wine was California Almadén Grenache Rosé. Afterwards they saw, in the East Room, Helen Hayes starring in "The White House," a play by A. E. Hotchner that dramatized events in the lives of presidents and first ladies.

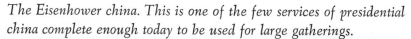

The Eisenhower china. This is one of the few services of presidential china complete enough today to be used for large gatherings.

Grant China
Fruit stand – French porcelain

The State Dining Room

The Grant china. Flowers in French porcelain fruit stand.

Top, table set for ten with George Washington china. Below, the Wilson china. To the left of each plate, individual menu card and matchbook marked "The President's House." (Luncheon for Senate wives, May 6, 1964)

The State Dining Room

*The Theodore Roosevelt china, part of a State dinner service made
by Wedgwood. Behind the identifying card was a Garfield French
porcelain compote. (Luncheon for Senate wives, May 6, 1964)*

100